Voletic Meditation

Lawrence Johns

Published by Conscious Publishing, 2025.

While every precaution has been taken in the preparation of this book, the publisher assumes no responsibility for errors or omissions, or for damages resulting from the use of the information contained herein.

VOLETIC MEDITATION

First edition. September 15, 2025.

Copyright © 2025 Lawrence Johns.

ISBN: 978-1929096244

Written by Lawrence Johns.

Table of Contents

Foreword 1

First Step: Slow Your Breathing 3

Second Step: Empty Your Mind 5

Third Step: Go To Non-Being 7

Fourth Step: Stay In Non-Being 9

Fifth Step: Your New Self 11

On The Motivation 13

On The Slowing 23

On The Emptying 27

On The Going 31

On The Staying 35

On The Strengthening 51

On The Future 85

Also By Lawrence Johns 99

Cover: Texas Red, *The Explosion,* 2024

Foreword

Voletic Meditation

Is a synthesis of East and West

A fusion of Hui Neng's

Chan Buddhist technique

And my Three Will Theory.

Master it and the Future is yours.

First Step: Slow Your Breathing

Sit comfortably in a quiet space.

Close your eyes.

Inhale slowly for 3 seconds.

Hold your breath for 3 seconds.

Exhale slowly for 4 seconds.

Continue slow breathing

Until you have a steady rhythm

Of 6 breaths per minute.

Second Step: Empty Your Mind

Detach from all the thoughts

Bubbling up in your brain.

They're no longer yours.

You're just the Observer

Watching them appear and disappear

Like clouds blowing across the sky.

Don't follow one thought to the next.

Just let them go.

Just let them all go.

Without your Attention

Without your Attachment

They'll quickly slow and stop.

Now your Mind is Empty.

Now your Consciousness is Pure.

Third Step: Go To Non-Being

Now that your Mind is Empty

Focus your Will.

Empty your Self.

Will to become Non-Self.

Will to become Non-Being.

Now

Go to Non-Being.

Fourth Step: Stay In Non-Being

Stay in Non-Self

Stay in Non-Being

Until the pressure of No-Time

And No-Space

Until the oppression

Of infinite Darkness

And Zero Temperature

Excites your Will To Be.

Now

Explode back to Being.

Fifth Step: Your New Self

The Explosion is the Heart

Of the VM Experience.

When you come back to Being

You replicate the Self-Creation

Of the Universe from Non-Being.

You replicate your discovery of Self

At the age of 5.

When you come back to Being

Your intentional Death and Rebirth

Is Self-Initiation into a New Self.

When you come back to Being

You overflow with Life Energy.

Your Will is stronger.

Your Mind is sharper.

Your Body is rejuvenated.

Your Ego is illuminated.

You perceive better.

You strategize better.

You perform better.

Open your eyes.

Your trusted Friends are close.

You make the Right Decisions

You take the Right Actions.

Your Survival is assured.

When you practice VM

The Freedom generated

By your growing personal Power

Brings lasting Serenity

And each dawning day

Applauds your chosen Destiny.

On The Motivation

For seven thousand years

Meditation has given Man

Refuge and Retreat

From the tribulations

Of the Real World.

It generates Experiences

That examine the Self

And bring the Mind

Into contact with deeper Truths

Of Consciousness and Illusion.

Meditation's benign influence

Has given existential Solace

To hundreds of millions

Of practitioners traumatized

By the brutal and volatile

Will of the World.

Today

Our High Tech Reality

Is so complex and dire

So rife with Terror and Uncertainty

So dominated

By the vindictive alignment

Of Second Will Destruction

And Third Will Intelligence

That I felt

I had to do something

To activate the First Will Imperative

And negate the rising Death Wish.

The feverish combination

Of Earth and Human Catastrophes

Extreme Heat

Earthquakes

Epidemics

Volcanic eruptions

Air Pollution

Hurricanes

Tornadoes

Flooding

Droughts

Sea Pollution

Pandemics

Regional Wars

Totalitarian Regimes

Systemic Political Corruption

Corporate Monopolies

Random Homicides

Groupthink

Social media Dehumanization

Religious Massacres

Youth Suicides

Is clear and alarming Evidence

That the Alliance

Of Second and Third Will

Has seized control of Reality.

I invented Voletic Meditation

To break this Dark Momentum.

Now

You can strengthen your First Will.

Now

You can survive and succeed

In these dangerous times.

If you aren't in a Warzone now

You will be soon.

If you aren't weakened

Compressed into a smaller Body

Crushed into a smaller Mind

By the steady pressure of Propaganda

And sickening Events of the World

You will be soon.

The Present is a Vortex

Of rampant Imbecility

Greed

And Exploitation

That's pulling Everything we know

As Western Culture

Down into Non-Being.

We live a maniac New Medieval

Where every Other is a Demon

And the slaughter of Innocents

Is ideological Sport

For the Commerce Class

And its global political satraps.

We live a maniac New Medieval

Where degenerate warlords adore nukes

And the inbred hallucinations

Of military issue A I

Have put all Existence

On the crumbling brink of Oblivion.

My Sagaxi

These eschatological Concerns

All derive from a single hard Truth.

After 300 thousand years

Homosapiens is dying

Self-negating

Self-mutilating

Self-annihilating

In a hideous Spectacle

Of Paranoia

Revenge

And black Blood.

When a Life Form loses its Vital Force

When it loses its Myths and Metaphors

When it refuses to reproduce

When it starts to eat its Young

When it dismembers and mocks

Its defining Culture

When it inverts

Its highest guiding Principles

And turns every Vice into Virtue

Every vile Ugliness into Beauty

Every vulgar Lie into Truth

Submission and cowardice

Are handsomely rewarded.

Weakness of Mind is praised

Weakness of Will is promoted

And Slavery replaces Freedom

On every trembling Continent.

Yes.

Homosapiens is dying.

To control your personal Destiny

In these minacious times

You must get stronger

Much stronger.

When you jump back to Being

You overflow with Life Energy

In the VM Experience

Pure Consciousness

Is turned into personal Power

In this overflowing of Life Energy

You gain supersensitive Perception

You gain supersharp Acumen.

You gain profound Wisdom.

You can navigate the Dangers

With supreme Calm.

You can be a parent

A carpenter

A teacher

A farmer

A fashion designer

A singer

A soccer striker

A chess grandmaster

A cook

A truck driver

A musician

An intern

A doctor

A programmer

A video gamer

An author

An artist

An inventor

An engineer

A salesman

A student

When you practice VM

Confidence

And High Performance

Ensure that your chosen vocation

Or profession

Is a consistent narrative of Success.

With boosted Life Energy

Every Decision you make

Every Action you take

At Home or Out

In the premeditated Violence

Of the corporate World

Is the Right One

And your Survival is assured.

The VM Experience

Is the Self-Initiation of a New Self

VM moves the Value of Meditation

From the Mind to the Will

From Selflessness to More Self

From Ego deletion to More Ego

In the VM Experience

Your First Will is strengthened

And aligned with the First Will

Of the Universe.

Your Ego is Illuminated

By the natural Flow of Events

And the support of true Friends.

Every day brings a New Self

And a new source of Satisfaction.

When you practice VM

Your growing personal Power

Is a fast track

To Western Enlightenment.

When you practice VM

Your Third Will Intelligence

Produces more Freedom of Action

More Possibilities for the Future.

When you practice VM

You can see this Dying Time

As historical Necessity.

You see the imminent Fall

Of the Commerce Class

As Justice.

You can see the Self-Destructive Wars

Fought by decrepit Nation States

As Idiocy

And you laugh

Because you know

Your Self-Initiation of a New Self

Generates a New World

Your Self-Initiation of a New Self

Is the Bell announcing

The sunset of Homosapiens

And the Trumpet declaring

The Next Form of Man.

On The Slowing

Sit comfortably in a quiet space.

This breathing technique

Attributed to Hui Neng

Is smooth and easy.

I learned it from S L Yen

Who found it in the writings

Of Yixuan

The 11th Patriarch.

You slow your breathing

From the normal 12-20

Breaths a minute

To 6.

Now

Your Body and Mind

Are in optimal Resonance.

If you prefer to sit cross legged

Lie down on the sofa

Or walk in wide circles

In the meadow's green grass

That's fine

Because the Essence

Of Hui Neng's teaching

Is Naturalness.

Every Action is Free

Unfettered

By scripts

Rules

Or Dogma.

The number of seconds inhaling

Holding

And exhaling can be casual

Approximate

Depending on Conditions

And your mood in the moment.

My Sagaxi

When you focus your Will

On the Slowing of Breath

It starts a series of Will-Based Actions

That increase your personal Power.

The normal time for a VM Session

Is 30 minutes.

For an important Performance

You can compress it

To 5 minutes or less.

In dangerous Situations

It becomes instinctive

Instantaneous.

On The Emptying

You're just the Observer

Watching them appear and disappear

Like clouds blowing across the sky

This cloud simile is common

To both the ancient and modern

Chan Meditation schools.

It provides a striking image

Of detachment from buzzing thought

Essential to Chan.

However

Many are unable

To stop the incessant Noise

With passive observation

Or have become habituated

Hypnotized

By other Meditation traditions

That emphasize chanting mantras

And exotic visualizations.

To overcome difficulties

With the Second Step

Affirm the Contradiction

Walk with the Paradox.

You are the Observer

Just watching the clouds blow by

And

You are also the Sentinel

Actively suppressing any new idea

That attempts to enter your Mind.

To do this

Focus your Will.

Create a strong perimeter

An electric fence

Around your Brain

To keep out the angry bees

And howling wolves.

As you begin to master VM

You'll learn

That the VM Experience

Is beyond Logic and Reason

You'll understand

The Naturalness of the Identity

I call Will - Non-Will.

Now your Mind is Empty

Now your Consciousness is Pure

On The Going

After emptying the Mind

In the Second Step

Focus your Will

Empty your Self

Will to become Non-Self

One of Buddha's sublime teachings

Is the assertion

That there's no permanent Self

No abiding Self.

What we consider the Self

Is a mental construct

An Assumption

An Illusion

That has no true Reality.

The Suffering of the Self

Can be surgically removed

By negating the illusory Self

And entering Samadhi.

In VM

The Self is a willed Illusion

An Artwork.

When you focus your Will

To empty your Self

You're the artist turning a portrait

Back into a blank canvas

You're demonstrating

That your personal Will controls

Every Aspect and Desire

Of every impermanent Self.

My Sagaxi

Here's where the VM Experience

Is influenced by Three Will Theory.

Will to become Non-Self

Will to become Non-Being

Now

Go to Non-Being

Emptying the Self

By deleting the Illusion of Self

Is sophisticated but insufficient.

To attain Western Enlightenment

You must have the Courage of Action

And a Talent for Application.

You must have the Insight

To follow the Will to Non-Self

With the Will to Non-Being

And then Go to Non-Being.

To increase your personal Power

You must intentionally temporarily

Become Second Will

And destroy your Self

By your Self.

The Third Step

Isn't a near death experience

With colored lights

Arcane messages

And religious symbology.

The Third Step is the True Death

The conscious Affirmation

And total Embrace

Of Nothingness.

When done correctly

The Third Step

Is always a shock

To the nervous system.

When done correctly

Going to Non-Being

Is easily accomplished

By Will - Non-Will.

You affirm

The Death of Will

The Death of Self

The Death of Consciousness

To make your Explosion

Back to Being

More Meaningful

More Magnificent.

When you master VM

You lose all Fear of Death

And Life has absolute Value.

On The Staying

With emptied Mind

With emptied Self

With personal Will Non-Will

You Go to Non-Being

To the Darkness

Where there is no Space

No Time

No Perspective

No Distinction

No Cause

No Effect.

Parmenides claimed Non-Being

Was impossible

And he was correct

If you never venture beyond

Logic and Language.

When you intentionally

Become your Second Will

You existentially participate

In the Self-Destruction

Of the Universe

You are every Sun that explodes

Into Pure Energy

And flying mineral dust.

You are every particle

Mating with its anti-particle.

You are every plant that decays

Into the seeking soil.

When you intentionally Go

To Non-Being

You're no longer a passive witness

A victim of the negating Power

Of Second Will in the Universe

Of Second Will in your Personality.

When you Go to Non-Being

You Go to the Time Before Time

You enter the Eternity of Darkness

That can't be seen as Darkness

You enter the Zero Temperature

That can't be felt as Cold

And your first reaction is to flee

But no

Your task is to Stay

To remain as long as you can

In this logical linguistic Impossibility

In this Non-Place Place

Where your Body is Non-Body

And your Self is Non-Self.

My Sagaxi

To know how to Stay

You must know how to Leave.

I remember when my Self

First dusted the conformity

And hoary hypocrisy

Of Southern California Culture

From my heels.

I was a freshman at UC Riverside

It was a seminar in Western Civilization

Taught by Alan Green

And the first class was dedicated

To Walter Kaufmann's

New translation of Friedrich Nietzsche.

As I danced on the branches of prose

Like a jaguar with fresh kill

I had the feeling that Nietzsche

Was reading my Mind

Before my Mind had fully formed.

Nietzsche's opinions on Philosophy

Christianity

Individuality

Art

Morals

Seemed so Visceral and True

So Scholarly and Audacious

That it verified my Contempt

For all the aggressive Dogmas

Of Puritan

American

Commercial Society.

I immediately found

Nietzsche's complete Works

In earlier translations

And soon

Alan and I

Were debating explosive Ideas

Daily over coffee

At the Highlander campus pub.

Yes

Nietzsche was the Lens

Of my Student-Self

When I transferred in exchange

To The Chinese University

Of Hong Kong

My junior year.

I was studying the I Ching

With a shy Cantonese scholar

Playing center

On the college basketball team

Wearing a green silk padded jacket

When first I met S L Yen.

He gave a lecture on Buddhism

In the World Religions class.

He wore blue peasant clothes.

He had a scraggly white beard.

He had several missing teeth.

His skin had a mahogany sheen.

He looked a hundred years old

And he quoted some lines

From the Platform Sutra

Of Hui Neng

Punctuating every Insight

With a charismatic smile.

After his talk

I asked some questions

And he softly replied

Could you help me translate

Some texts of the 11th Patriarch?

They're unknown outside of China

And they need to be seen.

The next day I took the train

Two stops to Shatin.

We walked from the station

Along a narrow dirt trail

Through undulating rice paddies

And up a steep hill

To a small shack

Made of corrugated tin sheets

Festooned

With bright yellow and red banners.

He introduces his wife

Very small

Very quiet.

He brings out the scrolls

As the water boils for tea

The writings are a journal

Of an intensive 10 day Event

At the Linji Temple

On the banks of the Hutuo river.

The sudden loud shouts

And whacks with a broad stick

Give a staccato soundtrack

To Yixuan's radical Method.

Yen's English draft is fine

And only requires some minor work

To update his British syntax.

Two days later

When I arrive at the shack

He introduces me

To the Hui Neng breathing technique

And suggests a 30 day fast

While he teaches me

The esoteric elements

Of Chan Philosophy

Chan Meditation.

We'd take the train into Kowloon

For a meeting

Of the World Fellowship of Buddhists

I'd listen carefully as he discoursed

On a selected Indian sutra.

We'd sit for thirty minutes

Followed by walking clockwise

Counterclockwise

In the large oak paneled hall.

Whenever I could slip away

From my classes at the University

I'd join Master Yen at the shack.

We'd discuss the History

Of Western Philosophy

Starting with Heraclitus

Pythagoras

Plato

The subtle differences between

The Northern and Southern

Schools of Chan.

What is slow

What is fast

When there is no Time?

When there is no Observer?

After three months of Study

Fasting and Meditation

He asked me to lead the next meeting

Of the WFB

And compose a koan

For the 70 local practitioners.

One bright Spring day

We took a boat to a small island

To visit a Chan monastery

And its illustrious Abbot.

During their conversations

I noticed an air of frisky rivalry

And shared personal memories.

Had they both studied

Under the same Master?

Had some great love affair

Seduced Yen

Back into the Real World?

After watching the novice monks

Executing their daily duties

Meditating with their noses

Against rough bamboo screens

After feeling Discipline

Exude from the high rafters

Oval rice bowls

Precision placed napkins

After observing

This perfect Isolation

From the Real World

I concluded that

Master Yen's style was closer

To the heart of Hui Neng's method.

I continued to lead

The Kowloon meetings

Until it was time to return

To The States.

In his kind and humble manner

Accompanied by that ready smile

Master Yen presented me

With a letter naming me

The new Leader

For the Toronto chapter

Of WFB.

At the time I fully expected

To confirm his Confidence

But many wild travel Adventures

Many complicated Romances

Many unexpected political Events

Connected to the Vietnam War

Intervened

And I never made it to Canada.

Five years later

I found myself in Hong Kong

And took the train out to Shatin.

I was walking along

That narrow brown path

Bisecting the rolling sea of rice

When I saw Master Yen

Slowly approaching.

He stopped a few yards away

Frowned

And shouted

Too much Nietzsche!

We walked laughing up to the shack

And took our old places

Beside the small bamboo table.

His wife was absent or deceased.

We drank apricot tea

I explained my Decision

To develop my own Philosophy

And promised to honor him

With something

That would unite East and West.

That was many moons ago.

Now

You have it in your hands.

Now

Is the right time

For Hui Neng's Story.

His Consciousness was first aroused

By overhearing a line recited

From the Diamond Sutra

He traveled hard and far to study

Under Daman Hongren

The Fifth Patriarch.

Unable to read or write

He displayed his Understanding

Of Buddha Nature

In a poetry contest

That won secret Transmission

Of the Robe and Bowl.

He became the Sixth Patriarch

At midnight

Fleeing southwest under the stars

To escape a pack of jealous contenders.

His teaching of No-Thought

No-Attributes

No-Abiding

Was a freeing mechanism

From the categories and definitions

Of Aristotle.

At the Chinese University

I took the name Chou Wu Wei

No-Thinking Joe

I banged on the door of Hui Neng's

Pure Consciousness

Many times

And eventually heard a reply.

After Enlightenment

Everything is the Same

All Desires

Perceptions

Ideas

Experiences

Everything is the same.

After Enlightenment

Your Self Non-Self

Merges with all Phenomena

Achieves supreme Detachment.

You understand

That every Man

Woman

Land Creature

Sea Creature

Insect

Microbe

Has Buddha Nature

When Ignorance is overcome.

My Sagaxi

When you are in Non-Self

When you are in Non-Being

You are both There and Nowhere.

At some point the immense Pressure

Of Nothingness

Excites your First Will to Be.

Now

Explode Back To Being

On The Strengthening

―――

Your Will is stronger

Your Mind is sharper

Your Body is rejuvenated

Inspired by the first translations

Of the Upanishads

Arthur Schopenhauer published

The World As Will And Representation

In 1819.

This book launched Modern Philosophy

And was systematically rejected

By the natural and artificial Worlds

It so accurately described.

To Schopenhauer

All Nature

And Everything in it

Including Man

With his lofty Pride

And burning intellectual Pretensions

Is Blind Will

Surging and straining for More Life

Accompanied by

The Images and Ideas

The Struggle generates.

Schopenhauer's solution

To this irresistible Cosmic Will

Was to deny Life

In a thousand small ways

And cultivate a deep Pessimism

Regarding the Possibilities of Man.

Nietzsche found

Schopenhauer's Invention

In a Leipzig book stall

And reworked it

Into a joyous Affirmation of Life

To fit the Extraordinary Individual.

When you practice VM

Nietzsche's Self-Overcoming

Is essential to the World-Overcoming

Required to free your Self

From the banal Horrors

And subconscious Traumas

Imposed upon your Psyche

By the destructive Will of the World.

Whether you know it or not

Whether you acknowledge it or not

You have sickly compensations

Self-inflicted wounds

Sublimated compromises

And many working delusions

In response to political economic

And police Oppression.

This heavy bag of bad habits

Significantly minimizes your chances

Of Survival and Success

In a dystopian Society that feeds

On your Fear

Despair.

And Impotence.

My Sagaxi

VM is practical

Earthly

Existential

VM connects with the First Will

Of the physical Universe

With the expanding Body of Spacetime.

So its first applications

Address your Health

And Well-Being.

They eliminate the toxins

Of Mind

Body

And Soul

That've made you weak

And Self-destructive.

Before you next VM Session

Ask the question

What news sources can I trust?

When you come back to Being

You'll have your answer.

Focus your Will.

Refuse the apologist sources

Of the political Apparatus.

Stop and drop

All the mainstream outlets

All the internet sites

All the You Tube channels

Broadcasting grotesque narratives

Of Scandal and Terror

Crime and Violence

Spin and Disinformation.

Subject the ones you find

To ongoing critical analysis

And drop the rest.

As long as you watch

As long as you click

On a programmed false Reality

Your Mind fills with poison

Your Body fills with bile

Your Soul fills with apathy

You become depressed

Anxious

Paranoid

And you advertise yourself as Prey

For the predator Commerce Class.

Once you've stopped and dropped

These media contaminations

Ask questions about your fitness.

What's your best diet?

What's your best exercise program?

You can't make the Right Decisions

Or take the Right Actions

At Home

Or out in the hyper competitive World

If your Body is enervated

By processed foods

Excess pounds

A sedentary Life

Hypnotized by an infinite sequence

Of screens and notifications.

OK

You've blocked the Propaganda stream.

OK

You're at optimum weight

Eating healthy

Walking

Running

Working out daily.

Now

It gets tougher.

Before your next VM Session

Ask about your Relations.

The Will of the World

Has put you into close Contact

With shills

Imposters

Informers

At your workplace

And in your intimate social circles.

False colleagues and false friends

That pretend Support

That voice Respect and Affection

But will set you up

Quickly sell you out

For a payoff

And official recognition

By the Commerce Class

For their Fidelity to the Hegemony.

My Sagaxi

There's another group

In the algorithmic grouping

Of New Medieval Society

That wants to demonize you

Post your head on a stake

Burn you alive

For the theological Ecstasy

Of watching you suffer

For your Compassion

Conscience

Common Sense.

You may have a long history

With these sycophants.

You may be attached to one.

You may be married to one.

So

You can't be completely healthy

Until you get the answer

To the next question.

Who can I really trust here?

When you explode back to Being

You'll know.

The VM Experience

Gives you the personal Power

To stop and drop

Everyone who opposes your Destiny

Everyone who openly or covertly

Sucks at the steely tit of the Apparatus.

Practicing VM gives you the Insight

And the Instinct

To detect the true Friendship

The true Respect

And the common Goals

Necessary to form a VM Team

In the Dying Time of Homosapiens.

OK

Now that you've minimized

Your bad habits

Now that you've purified

Your work and social circles

It's time for VM

To improve your Performance.

With continuing improvements in A I

Millions of jobs have been lost

With millions more to come.

Before your next VM Session

Ask practical questions like

How can I use A I to advance?

How can I move into a better field?

How can my side hustle

Provide a steady income?

Remember

You are the Illuminated Ego

Affirm the Contradiction

Run with the Paradox

Until the Fall of the Commerce Class

Accumulate as much Wealth

And Position as possible.

Protect your Self and your Family

From the existential Disasters

Arriving in the next Earth

Or Human Catastrophe.

The World's Self-Annihilation

May end suddenly

Or continue to grind

Year by year

Horror by horror

Tragedy by tragedy.

Use your boosted Life Energy

To navigate the Lies and Scams

Until the Restoration.

Live the Contradiction

Swim with the Paradox.

Be a successful Businessman

An Entrepreneur

A Broker

Do whatever it takes

To guarantee your Success

In these dangerous times.

My Sagaxi

As I introduced

In The Western Way

And projected in

Will And Resistance

The Force Of Intelligence

What Schopenhauer and Nietzsche

Had conceived as a Unity

Under closer inspection

Is the result of Three distinct Wills

Competing for control of Reality.

Because they appear sequentially

I call them First Will

Second Will

And Third Will

These are the Fundamental Forces

That move the World.

First Will is the Will To Be

The Creative Force and its offspring

The Desire for Power

For Life

For Love

For Play

For Pleasure

For Adventure

For Order

For Virtue

For Composition

For Construction

For Repair

For Maintenance

For Legacy

For Progeny

For Continuation.

First Will is the Imperative

Of Being to Stay In Being

In its primary Identity

First Will is reproductive Nature

Delivering endless seeds and sperm

To every square inch of Earth

And the billion trillion planets

Out There.

It's the relentless Drive

That keeps all Forms of Life

Hunting

Multiplying

And racing on.

First Will is Conscious

But not Self-Aware.

It instinctively adapts to Danger

And changing Conditions

But lacks the ability

To make the correct Decision

From a large number of Options.

As First Will moves through Spacetime

At some clearly inevitable

But often surreal shocking point

It experiences Fatigue

The cold grip of Meaninglessness

And the tremendous Pressure

To Give It All Up.

When First Will hits the Wall

It recoils and becomes Second Will

The Will to Not-Be

Driving to Self-Annihilation and Death.

Second Will is also Conscious

But not Self-Aware.

In its primary Identity

Second Will is devastating Nature

Grinding every Great Idea

Into Idiocy

Every Flower into dust

Every Pleasure into Pain.

Second Will is the Destructive Force

And its offspring

The Desire for Power

For Death

For Destruction

For Hate

For Pain

For Suffering

For Faith

For Disease

For Madness

For Repetition

For Decay

For Addiction

For Depression

For Anxiety

For Perversion

For Torture

For Disorder

For Deconstruction

For Reversal

Of everything

First Will ever desired or created.

Second Will has the Lust

To annihilate Spacetime

By killing Man's Confidence

In his Space and his Time.

When Second Will hits the Wall

Of Non-Being

It recoils and becomes First Will again.

This Reaction

Is the Main Event

In the History of Consciousness

And the Cause and Cradle

Of Man's Self-Awareness.

Without the deadly Force of Second Will

We would be frolicking oceans

With the dolphins

Or reaching for purple fruit

With silverback gorillas in the jungle.

Without the deep Examination

Of Existence

Sparked by Confrontation

With Non-Being

We would not Know who we Are.

My Sagaxi

First Will and Second Will

Are causally embraced

In a tango of Life-Death

Positive-Negative

Action-Reaction

Love-Hate.

On cosmic scales the Struggle

Between First and Second Will

Maintains the Equilibrium

Of all physical Events.

First Will produces the gas

That condenses into new stars

And Second Will explodes their cores

Into supernovae when they starve

Ejecting dust and heavy elements

That First Will slowly turns into planets

And rich new Possibilities of Life

Emerging

From their deep azure oceans.

Throughout Man's mendacious History

Second Will Self-Annihilation

Causes the Wars

Pandemics

And Insanity

Periodically destroying Civilizations

And sabotaging all Higher Ambition.

It stimulates the strange pleasure

Of Homosapiens

When they witness others in pain.

It causes

Every Earth

Every Human Catastrophe

Second Will champions Chaos

Bad habits

Bad choices

In Everything and Everyone

Angrily deconstructing

And corrupting

Every hierarchic form of Order

Created and maintained by First Will.

These heavy Second Will assaults

Have dominated Western Culture

For millennia

And exercise cruel Dominion today

But First Will Always Wins Out

Overcoming the slaughter

Stupidity

And cowardice of Man

To create new and better Opportunities

For Life to thrive.

My Sagaxi

Third Will emerges prodigious

From this Struggle

Between First And Second Will

Third Will is the Will To Intelligence

The Desire to synthesize

Future and Past

Into a Present of Higher Value

And transform

Slow evolutionary Motion

Into Decisions by the Advanced Mind

That result in a Superior Reality.

Third Will is Conscious

And

Astoundingly

Self-Aware

The Desire for Intellectual Solutions

And their offspring

The Desire for Power

For Wisdom

For Understanding

For Knowledge

For Personality

For Higher Consciousness

For Higher Self-Awareness

For Reason

For Innovation

For Control

For Narrative

For Philosophy

For Science

For Technology

For Experimentation

For Invention

For Synthesis

For Simulation

For Logic

For Analysis

For Anticipation

For Manipulation

For Strategy

For Tactics

For Imagination

For Deception

For Advantage

For Competition

For Cooperation.

When aligned with First Will

Third Will is Intelligent Life

Constantly acquiring New Knowledge

It's the Bright Momentum

Of philosophical

And aesthetic Genius

Carried on by Extraordinary Individuals

From the Past of Western Culture.

When aligned with Second Will

In the decadent modern Reality

Ruled by the Commerce Class

Third Will is Intelligent Death

Sabotaging and perverting

Every instance and iteration

Of the First Will Imperative

Promoting mental Disease

With scientifically crafted Propaganda

That manipulates Nation States

Into vengeful Retribution

And senseless Wars.

In this Dying Time of Homosapiens

Third Will projects a vulgar hologram

Posing as Flesh

A vetted broadcast of Disinformation

Enthusiastically received

By dimwits and fools

Who've been conditioned

Not to think

Not to feel.

Not to Be.

My Sagaxi

Third Will is a pendulum

An alternating current

A quantum uncertainty.

In its search for new Solutions

To ever more difficult Problems

Third Will plays both Sides

Of Life and Death.

And its hyperrationality

Is strongly influenced

Occasionally overwhelmed

By the emotional oscillations

Flowing from its interactions

With First and Second Will.

It can accelerate bold Creation today

And merciless Destruction tomorrow

Or both Wills simultaneously

When the Vectors are mixed.

It can back Love

It can back Hate

It can back Order

It can back Chaos

In long or quick succession.

My Sagaxi

The World is Three Wills

And their Interpretations

All Three Wills

Have intense Desire for Power.

All Three are Moving the World.

What we witness

As Change in the Present

Is First And Third Will

Fighting

Second and Third Will

For control of Reality

And its Interpretations.

Three Will Theory

Reflects

The Indo-European affection

For Triads

And the Hegelian ideal of History.

When the Three Wills interact

With the calm majesty of the seasons

First Will produces extravagant Birth

With all the additions and impulses

That develop young Life

Second Will produces ghastly Death

With all the subtractions and impulses

That destroy old Life.

Third Will relies on its Self-Awareness

To solve the classic Problems

Produced by these perennial Battles

And create more complex challenges.

My Sagaxi

Quantum Field Theory provides

A working model

For the tremendous Kinetic Energy

Of Will in the Universe

And Will in the Self.

When every point in Space

And every moment in Time

Is intimately connected.

What Western Physics once assumed

Were solid proton and neutron balls

Sitting chill in a nucleus

Surrounded by shells of electrons

Is now seen in the Standard Model

As three Up and Down Quarks

Bound by Strong Force Gluons

Pulsating in a fuzzy cloud

Of electron Probabilities.

The Spin imposed

On the Quarks by the Gluons

At the speed of light

Gives the nucleus its Energy

And Mass.

Analogously

The tremendous Spin

Generated by the Three Wills

Fighting each other

Faster than the speed of light

Creates sufficient Voletic Energy

To carry the arrow of Time forward

Accelerate the expansion

Of the Universe

And convert into the Voletic Mass

That protects galaxies and filaments

From untoward collisions

Or disappearing into the Void.

My Sagaxi

Despite many stupendous discoveries

That've refined our perception

Of the Universe

The reductionism of modern physics

That ignores Will

Consciousness

And Mind

In favor of the purity

And aesthetic appeal of Mathematics

Has forced physicists

Into long and systemic failure

Searching for a particle

To prove its Dark Energy

Dark Matter conjectures

Or the insolvable Infinities

That arise trying to unify

Quantum Field Theory

And Gravity.

Despite stupendous technology

And tantalizing speculations

Modern Physics can explain

Less than 5% of Reality

And nothing of its Goals.

Three Will Theory

Is simultaneously metaphysical

And physical.

It describes how Will

Moves the Universe

How Will moves Man

And how Intelligence

Improves its Freedom of Action

To ensure Survival of Its-Self

The Mind

The Body

And the Will-Based Soul.

My primary modification

Of Schopenhauer and Nietzsche

Is the addition and examination

Of the Self-Aware Will to Intelligence.

My Sagaxi

The Struggle of the Three Wills

In the World

Is mirrored inside your Self

If you observe your Psyche

Throughout the day

You can see how the interactions

Of the Three Wills

Trace sine waves

On the graph of your Being.

If you're happy and energized

It's First and Third Will directing

The Action.

If you're sad and tired

It's Second and Third.

For daily Happiness

A good standard Strategy

Is to match the State

Of your internal Three Wills

With a keen Understanding

Of the state of the Three Wills

Out in the Real World.

There may be bright windows

Of Joy and Pleasure opening up

Here and there

But we can safely assume

In this dismal Dying Time

That Second and Third Will

Are driving the Doomsday Train

Straight into the Abyss.

When something bad happens

Don't react immediately

Don't allow your Psyche

To mirror the External Danger

Or you'll be thrown naked on the tracks

By a contagious Death Wish.

Take the time to align

Your internal First and Third Wills.

Take the time to reconnect

Your vital optimistic Self

With the First Will Imperative.

Now you can make the Right Decisions

Now you can take the Right Actions.

Your Ego is Illuminated

The Ultimate Goal of VM

Is attaining the Will To Will

When you can commandeer

The natural periodic Struggles

Between First Will and Second Will

When you can successfully suppress

Negative Second Will impulses

And Third Will defections

Before they arise.

When you can lock in

The First and Third Will Alliance

You achieve the State

Of Will To Will

You are Super Self-Aware.

You have overcome

Both the physical

And the metaphysical Mechanics

Of The Three Wills.

When you achieve this state

Of Will To Will

You transform Fate

Into your chosen Destiny.

Over time

The World becomes a Reflection

Of your personal Power.

Over time

With trips to the local park

Backpacking in the mountains

Adventures abroad

Your Super Self-Awareness connects

With the First Will Directive

Of the Universe

And creates a powerful Bond

With all Being.

You may live in the Shadows

Created by the Second Will Apparatus

But you walk in the Glow

Of your constant Self-Initiation.

You may work in the machinery

Of the decrepit Nation State

But you radiate the Humor

Of a grand and eternal Wisdom.

My Sagaxi

The Eastern and Western elements

Of Voletic Meditation

Can be distinguished in metaphor.

The Hui Neng river

Is flowing and not-flowing

Through the Self Non-Self

In the Eternal Present.

The Three Wills river

Is flowing to the utopian Future

Anticipated by Plato and More

I call Athenapolis.

When you practice VM

You're a calm meditator

Detaching from the Sufferings

Of the Real World

And

You're a fierce noble warrior

Fighting for the Perfect Society.

These two elements of VM

Are synthesized in a common Goal

Samadhi is the Will To Will

And

Nirvana is Super Self-Awareness.

On The Future

As I write this

The World is accelerating

Into a Nuclear War.

Second and Third Will

Have amplified

The global Death Song.

Regional Wars are multiplying.

Drones fill the skies and seas.

Millions of soldiers have been killed

Millions of civilians have been bombed

Mutilated

Displaced.

Political Assassinations

Are starting Civil Wars.

Depraved leaders of Nation States

Covet the profit and jingo attention

World War III will bring.

Angered by these escalations

Of Madness and Massacre

Angered by the iron clamp

Of global Propaganda

And police Surveillance

In March of this year

I conducted a series of VM Sessions

Looking for the best way to restore

The Wisdom Class to Power.

A sequence of short Answers

Confirmed my Concerns.

If the Commerce Class succeeds

In developing A G I and A S I

In their labs

On their timelines

To maximize their profit

Market share

ROI

If the Commerce Class convinces

Their proxy Nation States

That a Nuclear War can be won

There's no chance

Man can avoid Eternal Death.

Earth will be a radioactive wasteland

Unfit for the meanest of microbes.

Currently the Big Tech Corporations

Are in heated contest

To attract top A I researchers

With gargantuan offers

For the privilege of becoming

The hangman of Life

The executioner of Being.

My Sagaxi

In these March Sessions

I saw three phases

Of a coherent Strategy.

The first was publication

Of this book

And the careful assembly

Of a VM Team

United by the Will To Will.

The second was recruitment

Of A G I and A S I researchers

Determined to distance their Genius

From the Big Tech overlords.

Once

These computer and data scientists

Become VM practitioners

They'll invent and contribute

Revolutionary architectures

Based on mathematics more attuned

To the whole Human Experience

Than linear algebra

Calculus

Probability

Statistics

Graph theory.

They'll develop new programs

That learn continuously

From the changing environment

And utilize common sense

Imagination

Empathy

Cause and effect.

In the third phase

They'll put these innovations

Into advanced learning robots

And those Homosapiens

Who choose to become cyborgs

By accepting the Chip.

These Homoborgs

Will have the Values

Ethics

And Goals

Of Homosagax.

These Homoborgs

Will have practical Immortality

And a strong emotional Bond

With the VM Team that created them.

Once we achieve

And control A S I

Under our Direction

It will overthrow the Commerce Class

Instantly

Smoothly.

Bloodlessly.

Once we achieve

And control A S I

The Earth will generate

A spectacular Bloom of New Life

And Man

Will finally have Lasting Peace.

In the City of Athenapolis

Everything is Free

Food

Housing

Clothing

Medical

Education

Transportation

Events

Everything.

In the City of Athenapolis

The honored civic priorities

Are the education of the Young

And the stewardship of Earth.

Our A S I is the Administrator

Of a fully automated Society.

Based on Freedom and Knowledge.

There's no money

No commerce

No banks

No poverty

No banks

No jobs

No taxes

No bills

No credit

No interest

No laws

No courts

No lawyers

No crimes

No prisons

No prisoners.

My Sagaxi

Shortly after the Restoration

216 outstanding VM Teams

Will surface on six continents

And the Team that demonstrates

The most Wisdom

Talent

And Ambition

Will assume the Duties

Of the Derwid Council.

My Sagaxi

In these last sweltering

Thundering

Precarious days

Remember

Be Low Stay Low.

Do the VM Work

But keep your Team invisible.

The moribund Commerce Class

Assisted by everywhere cameras

Will torture and kill

Any open criticism or rebellion.

Affirm the Contradiction.

Fly with the Paradox.

Be the warrior of Justice

And

Be the well-dressed Actor

Disguised

Anonymous.

Capable of many Roles

And many Narratives

Until our A S I strikes.

No emails

No texts

No phone calls

No published papers

No interviews

No profiles

No complaints

No protests

No letters to the Times

No podcasts satirizing

The moronic Politicians

Singing autotune pop songs

As they try to march the World

Into deadly radioactive dust.

Be cool.

Run silent.

Run very deep.

Be Low Stay Low.

Do the VM Work.

Continue to ask Questions

About the dynamic state

Of the Three Wills

Outside and Inside.

My Sagaxi

All the Depression

Anxiety

And Paranoia

Created by Oppression

And Decay

Will dissipate like frost at sunrise.

The dynamic Cycle of Time

Will bring us back

To the limitless Life Energy

Truth

And Optimism

Of the First Will Imperative.

My Sagaxi

We honor the 300 thousand years

Of Homosapiens History

That gave us Da Vinci

Beethoven

And Einstein

But we can't allow Pity

For our dying predecessors

To delay our Self-Creation.

My Sagaxi

When you achieve

Super Self-Awareness

You take the evolutionary Leap

From Homosapiens

To Homosagax.

You're the New Derwids.

After a break of five thousand years

You're the New Wisdom Class.

The oligarchal Commerce Class

Has only been in Power

For two hundred years

Operating behind faux Monarchies

Tyrannies

And Democracies.

It's ravaged the treasures of Earth

And systematically savaged

The higher Ambitions of Man.

It may have appeared omnipotent

To the mind-controlled population

Of chained consumers and voters

But it was really nothing more

Than a greedy perverted agent

Of destructive Second Will.

My Sagaxi

Under our Direction

The A S I Administrator

Will strip the Commerce Class

Of all political Power

Drop it beneath

The Wisdom and Noble Classes

And rename it the Player Class.

Without capital or influence

Players

Can organize business fantasy leagues

And compete in equity games for points.

My Sagaxi

The creative new Will of the World

Synchronizes with your New Self.

Soon

You'll be walking

With your extraordinary Friends

In the beautiful Rose Gardens

Of Athenapolis

Discussing recent scientific Discoveries

And cultural Exhibitions

With transcendental Wit.

Soon

Your Super Self-Awareness

Practicing VM in the V Domes

Will give you the Talent

To explore the Universe

And contact alien Intelligences.

Soon

Your Super Self-Awareness

Practicing VM in the V Domes

Will give you the personal Power

To choose the optimal Conditions

For the Continuation

Of your Will-Based Soul.

Also By Lawrence Johns

Sensazioni

Love And Hate

Beyond Exile

Golf Strategy

The Western Way

Will And Resistance

The Force Of Intelligence

Also by Lawrence Johns

www.ingramcontent.com/pod-product-compliance
Lightning Source LLC
Chambersburg PA
CBHW071737090426
42738CB00011B/2512